FULFILLMENT
of
BIBLICAL PROPHECY

Reverend S Elbert Gaffney

xulon
PRESS

FOREWORD

WRITING OF THIS "FULFILLMENT OF BIBLICAL PROPHECY" STUDY GUIDE WAS BEGUN IN 1980. ALTHOUGH IT WAS DIVINELY INSPIRED, IT WAS PUT ASIDE OVER A PERIOD OF YEARS IN FAVOR OF OTHER PRIORITIES. HOWEVER, IN 2011 THE LORD RENEWED MY ZEAL AND FERVOR, AND ALLOWED COMPLETION OF THIS MANUSCRIPT TO HAPPEN IN 2013.

IT IS HIGHLY RECOMMENDED THAT THIS BOOK BE USED AS A "SIGNS OF THE END TIMES" STUDY GUIDE.

TO GOD BE ALL THE GLORY!!!

REVEREND S. ELBERT GAFFNEY,
AUTHOR

ACKNOWLEDGMENT

My sincerest appreciation goes to my former pastor, Reverend Reynold C. Carr; an outstanding "Expository Teacher" of God's Word and a personal mentor to me during his tenure as my pastor!

REVEREND S. ELBERT GAFFNEY

INTRODUCTION

- *THIS "FULFILLMENT OF BIBLICAL PROPHECY"*

STUDY GUIDE INVOLVES:

THE BOOK OF DANIEL   *CHAPTER 2*
                                   CHAPTER 7

CROSS-REFERENCED WITH THE BOOKS OF: MATTHEW, MARK, LUKE, AND REVELATION...

THE BOOK OF DANIEL CONTAINS A VARIETY OF PROPHETIC TRUTHS; HOWEVER THIS STUDY GUIDE DOES NOT ATTEMPT TO ENCOMPASS ALL OF THEM, BUT RATHER WILL FOCUS UPON TWO AREAS:

(1) NEBUCHADNEZZAR'S DREAM OF THE GREAT IMAGE (DANIEL 2:1)...

(2) DANIEL'S DREAM AND VISIONS OF THE FOUR BEASTS (DANIEL 7:1-14, 23-27).

- *IN THE <u>DREAM</u>; NEBUCHADNEZZAR SAW A HUGE AND POWERFUL STATUE OF A MAN. IT'S HEAD WAS GOLD, IT'S BREAST AND ARMS WERE SILVER, IT'S BELLY AND THIGHS WERE BRASS, IT'S LEGS WERE IRON; AND FEET PART IRON AND PART CLAY. THIS STATUE WAS THEN UTTERLY PULVERIZED INTO SMALL POWDER BY A SPECIAL ROCK, SUPERNATURALLY CUT FROM A MOUNTAINSIDE, WHICH FELL UPON IT...THE ROCK THEN GREW UNTIL IT FILLED THE ENTIRE EARTH (DANIEL 2:31-35, REVELATION 16:19).*

- *THIS STUDY GUIDE ALSO INCLUDES THE "BIRTH AND RAPTURE" OF THE CHURCH (THE CHURCH AGE)... AND JESUS' OLIVET DISCOURSE (MATTHEW 24: 1-51).*

SCOPE OF STUDY

1. THE GENTILE INTERLUDE
2. THE CHURCH AGE
3. JESUS' OLIVET DISCOURSE

LEARNING GOAL

THIS STUDY IS DESIGNED TO: *(1)* CORRELATE PROPHETIC SCRIPTURE WITH SECULAR HISTORY AND *(2)* EVALUATE *"SIGNS OF THE END TIMES"* IN THE LIGHT OF PRESENT DAY WORLD DEVELOPMENTS *(SIGNS OF THE TIMES, H.L. WILMINGTON)*.

THE BABYLONIAN CAPTIVITY

- DANIEL, WHOSE NAME MEANS *"GOD IS MY JUDGE"*, WAS TAKEN IN HIS YOUTH TO BABYLON, ALONG WITH HIS THREE COMPANIONS (HANANIAH, MISHAEL AND AZARIAH), IN THE FIRST DEPORTATION, UNDER KING NEBUCHADNEZZAR (DANIEL 1:1,3,6,7).
- DANIEL SOON EXCELLED IN WISDOM IN THE LAND, FAMOUS FOR IT'S WISE MEN, AND ULTIMATELY ROSE TO BECOME FIRST AMONG THE THREE HIGHEST OFFICERS OF THE MEDO-PERSIAN EMPIRE (DANIEL 5:29; 6:1-3).
- DANIEL'S LIFE IN BABYLON EXTENDED TO AT LEAST 530 B.C. (SCOFIELD BIBLE; pg 896).

CONTENTS

THE GENTILE INTERLUDE

- DANIEL, CHAPTERS TWO AND SEVEN, DESCRIBE THE PERIOD OF TIME NAMED BY CHRIST IN LUKE 21:24, AS "THE TIMES OF THE GENTILES".

- THE "TIMES OF THE GENTILES" BEGAN WITH THE CAPTIVITY OF JUDAH UNDER KING NEBUCHADNEZZAR (2 CHRONICLE 36:1-21)...

- SINCE WHICH TIME JERUSALEM HAS BEEN UNDER GENTILE OVERLORDSHIP (SCOFIELD BIBLE, pg 1106).

- THE TIMES OF THE GENTILES IS "THE GENTILE INTERLUDE" WHEN DAVID IS NOT ON THE THRONE, AND THE JEWS ARE UNDER THE DOMINION OF THE GENTILE NATIONS...

- IT BEGAN WITH THE "BABYLONIAN CAPTIVITY" (606 B.C., DANIEL 1:1,3,6-7), AND WILL END WITH THE SECOND COMING OF CHRIST; WHEN HE SETS UP HIS EARTHLY KINGDOM (DANIEL 2:44; 7:14, MATTHEW 24:29-30, MARK 13:26, REVELATION 19:16).

- THE SAINTS REFERRED TO ARE THE JEWISH REMNANT, WHO ARE NOW "SCATTERED" AMONG THE NATIONS (ZECHARIAH 1:19) ARE BEING REGATHERED, AND WILL BE HATED BY THE LITTLE HORN, THE ANTI-CHRIST; WHO WILL SEEK TO DESTROY THEM (DANIEL 7:7, 8; REVELATION 13:1).

- THEY WILL BE DELIVERED BY CHRIST, RESTORED AS A NATION AND RULED BY CHRIST! (DANIEL 7:9).

Note! "The Millennial Reign" (Daniel 7:9, 13, 14, 22, 27, Revelation 20:4).

NEBUCHADNEZZAR'S DREAM OF THE GREAT IMAGE

- *IN THE SECOND YEAR OF THE REIGN OF KING NEBUCHADNEZZAR, HE DREAMED DREAMS... WAS TROUBLED IN HIS SPIRIT, AND HIS SLEEP WENT FROM HIM (DANIEL 2:1)...*

- *IN THE DREAM, NEBUCHADNEZZAR SAW A HUGE AND POWERFUL STATUE OF A MAN (DANIEL 2:31)...*

- *IT WAS MADE UP OF VARIOUS KINDS OF MATERIALS: IT'S HEAD WAS GOLD, IT'S BREAST AND ARMS WERE SILVER, IT'S BELLY AND THIGHS WERE BRASS... IT'S LEGS WERE IRON, AND IT'S FEET PART IRON AND PART CLAY (DANIEL 2:32, 33)...*

- *THE STATUE WAS THEN UTTERLY PULVERIZED INTO SMALL POWDER BY A SPECIAL ROCK, SUPERNATURALLY CUT FROM A MOUNTAINSIDE, WHICH FELL UPON IT...*

- *THE ROCK THEN GREW UNTIL IT FILLED THE ENTIRE EARTH, (DANIEL 2:34, 35, 44, 45).*

_____

_____

_____

_____

_____

_____

_____

_____

_____

_____

_____

_____

_____

NEBUCHADNEZZAR'S COMMAND AND DECREE

- *...THEN THE KING GAVE THE "COMMAND" TO CALL THE MAGICIANS, THE ASTROLOGERS, THE SORCERERS, AND THE CHALDEANS; TO TELL THE KING HIS DREAMS...SO THEY CAME AND STOOD BEFORE THE KING (DANIEL 2:2) HOWEVER; **NONE** OF THE MAGICIANS, ASTROLOGERS, SORCERERS OF CHALDEANS COULD INTERPRET KING NEBUCHADNEZZAR'S DREAM (DANIEL 2:10, 11)...*

- *FOR THIS REASON THE KING WAS ANGRY AND VERY FURIOUS, AND GAVE THE COMMAND TO DESTROY ALL THE WISE MEN OF BABYLON (DANIEL 2:12).*

- *SO THE "DECREE" WENT OUT, AND THEY BEGAN KILLING THE WISE MEN...AND THEY SOUGHT DANIEL, AND HIS THREE COMPANIONS (HANANIAH, MISHAEL AND AZARIAH) TO KILL THEM ALSO (DANIEL 2:13, 17).*

- *WHEN ARIOCH, THE COMMANDER OF THE KING'S GUARD, HAD GONE OUT TO PUT TO DEATH THE WISE MEN OF BABYLON, DANIEL SPOKE TO HIM WITH WISDOM AND TACT (V. 14)... HE ASKED THE KING'S OFFICER, "WHY DID THE KING ISSUE SUCH A HARSH DECREE?" **ARIOCH THEN EXPLAINED THE MATTER TO DANIEL (DANIEL 2:15).***

- *SO DANIEL WENT IN AND ASKED THE KING TO GIVE HIM TIME...THAT HE MIGHT TELL THE KING THE INTERPRETATION (DANIEL 2:16)...*

- ***THEN WAS THE SECRET REVEALED TO DANIEL IN A NIGHT VISION (DANIEL 2:17-19A)...***

SO DANIEL BLESSED THE GOD OF HEAVEN (DANIEL 2:19B)!

_____

_____

_____

_____

_____

_____

DANIEL'S VISION OF THE FOUR BEASTS

- *DANIEL SAW VICIOUS ANIMALS FIGHTING WITH EACH OTHER… ONE WAS LIKE A LION, THE SECOND LIKE A BEAR, AND THE THIRD LIKE A LEOPARD, WHILE THE FOURTH (THE MOST HORRIBLE OF ALL) WAS SOMEWHAT OF A COMPOSITE OF THE FIRST THREE… AND IT HAD TEN HORNS (DANIEL 7:1-7)…*

- *I CONSIDERED THE HORNS AND BEHOLD, THERE CAME UP AMONG THEM ANOTHER LITTLE HORN (DANIEL 7:8), BEFORE WHOM THERE WERE THREE OF THE FIRST HORNS PLUCKED UP BY THE ROOTS: AND BEHOLD IN THIS HORN WERE EYES LIKE THE EYES OF MAN AND A MOUTH SPEAKING GREAT THINGS.*

- *AT THE END OF THIS VISION DANIEL SAW A MIGHTY FIGURE FROM HEAVEN, WHO DESTROYED THESE BEASTS AND SET UP AN EVERLASTING KINGDOM UPON THE EARTH (DANIEL 7:9-14, 23-27).*

DANIEL'S INTERPRETATION OF NEBUCHADNEZZAR'S DREAM

- *FROM NEBUCHADNEZZAR'S DREAM, AND DANIEL'S VISION, AND SECULAR HISTORY, WE LEARN THAT FOUR MAJOR POWERS WILL RULE OVER PALESTINE (JEWS)…BABYLON, MEDO-PERSIA, GREECE, ROME.*

- *THESE POWERS ARE VIEWED BY MANKIND AS (DANIEL 2:31-33):*
1. *GOLD,*
2. *SILVER,*
3. *BRASS,*
4. *IRON AND CLAY.*

- *THESE POWERS ARE VIEWED BY GOD AS FOUR WILD ANIMALS (DANIEL 7:3-8):*
1. *A WINGED LION,*
2. *A BEAR,*
3. *A WINGED LEOPARD,*
4. *AND AN INDESCRIBABLY BRUTAL AND VICIOUS ANIMAL.*

AS DANIEL DESCRIBES KING NEBUCHADNEZZAR'S "DREAM" AND GIVES THE INTERPRETATION HE EMPHASIZES THAT IT IS PROPHETIC

1. "LATTER DAYS" (DANIEL 2:28)
2. SHOULD COME TO PASS "HEREAFTER" (DANIEL 2:29)

NOTE!

- THE QUALITY OF GENTILE RULE DEGENERATES; AS INDICATED BY THE DIMINISHING VALUE OF THE METALS, AND BY THE INCREASING VICIOUS NATURE OF THE BEASTS...

- THE STRENGTH INCREASES AS THE QUALITY DECREASES.

- THE TOES OF THE HORNS (KINGS OF KINGDOMS) OF THE LAST BEAST OF THE "REVIVED ROMAN EMPIRE" (DANIEL 7:7)

- THE LITTLE HORN IS THE LAST WORLD RULER (DANIEL 7:8)...

- **HE WILL RULE OVER THE LAST "KINGDOM FORM" OF THE REVIVED ROMAN EMPIRE...**

- HE IS THE FIRST BEAST OF REVELATION 13:1, THE "MAN OF SIN" (THE ANTI-CHRIST) OF 2 THESSALONIANS 2:3...

- HE IS DESTROYED AT THE "SECOND COMING" OF CHRIST (2 THESSALONIANS 2:8) !

_____

_____

_____

_____

_____

_____

_____

WORLD EMPIRES WHICH SHALL RULE OVER THE JEWS

THE DREAM	THE VISION	THE SCRIPTURE
1. GOLD	LION	BABYLON	(DANIEL 2:36-38; 7:4)
2. SILVER	BEAR	MEDO-PERSIA	(DANIEL 2:39A; 7:5)
3. BRASS	LEOPARD	GREECE	(DANIEL 2:39B; 7:6)
4. IRON	TERRIBLE BEAST	ROME	(DANIEL 2:40-41; 7:1-14)

- IRON/CLAY -TEN HORNS/LITTLE HORN - *DIVIDED* KINGDOMS _____ (DANIEL 7:7,8)
- STONE __CHRIST_____ INVESTIGATIVE JUDGMENT/CHRIST'S KINGDOM
  (DANIEL 2:31-35, 44, 45; 7:14, 22-27; REVELATION: 11:15; 19:16)

PERIODS OF "EMPIRE RULE"

1. BABYLON _____ 625 B.C. TO 539 B.C.
2. MEDO-PERSIA _____ 539B.C. TO 331 B.C.
3. GREECE _____ 331 B.C. TO 323B.C.
4. **FOR ROME THREE PERIODS ARE TO BE NOTED:**

(1) THE FIRST PERIOD, THE ORIGINAL EMPIRE_300 B.C. -476 A.D.
(2) THE SECOND PERIOD, (THE INTERVENING INFLUENCE)... _476 A.D. –PRESENT.
(3) THE THIRD PERIOD (THE REVIVED EMPIRE) RAPTURE-ARMAGEDDON,
(1 THESSALONIANS 4:16-17, REVELATION 16:16)

THE REVIVED ROMAN EMPIRE

- **THE "REVIVED EMPIRE" WILL CONSIST OF TEN NATIONS**
                              (DANIEL 7:7, REVELATION 12:3, 13:1, 16:16).

- **THE ANTI-CHRIST (DANIEL 7:8) WILL "PERSONALLY" UNITE THESE NATIONS; BASED UPON THREE FACTORS:**
                              1. MILITARY
                              2. ECONOMIC
                              3. POLITICAL

Rome's Intervening Influence

1. World Church (Papacy)
2. Judicial Systems
3. Law, Medicine, Natural Science
4. Military Systems and Western Defense
5. **Organizations and Treaties**

   (1) League of Nations: Precursor to the U.N. (1920-1946)
   (2) Nato..North Atlantic Treaty Organization(April 4, 1949)
   (3) Treaty of Rome (March 25, 1957)
   (4) European common market (May 28, 1979)…European Monetary System (January 1, 1981)…E.U. Precursor.
   (5) **E.U… European Union,(Believed to be a precursor to the "Revived Roman Empire"…And the coming Anti-Christ (Daniel 7:7, 8).**

Christ's Statement

"And they shall fall by the edge of the sword, and be led away captive into all Nations…and Jerusalem shall be trodden down of the Gentiles, until "The times of the Gentiles, be fulfilled" (Luke 21:24).

Note!

Both, the history and prophecy of Christ's statement are explained by a "Dream" and a "Vision" in the Book of Daniel:
1. A Babylonian King had a "Dream" (Daniel 2:31-35)…
2. While Daniel saw the "Vision" (Daniel 7:1-14).

_____

_____

_____

_____

_____

GOD'S METHODS OF REVELATION TO NEBUCHADNEZZAR AND DANIEL

- *IT IS INTERESTING TO NOTE THAT GOD REVEALED THE SAME THINGS TO NEBUCHADNEZZAR AND DANIEL IN DIFFERENT WAYS:*

   1. *NEBUCHADNEZZAR, BEING A MATERIALISTIC MAN SAW ONLY THE EXTERNAL APPEARANCES OF THESE KINGDOMS, WHILE...*
   2. *DANIEL, BEING A SPIRITUAL MAN SAW THE TRUE NATURE OF THESE KINGDOMS.*

QUOTE!

- *... "FOR THE LORD SEETH NOT AS MAN SEETH: FOR MAN LOOKETH ON THE OUTWARD APPEARANCE, BUT THE LORD LOOKETH ON THE HEART" (1 SAMUEL 16:7).*

_____

_____

_____

_____

_____

_____

_____

_____

_____

_____

_____

_____

_____

_____

_____

_____

_____

THE CHURCH AGE

- *JESUS SAID UNTO PETER: "THOU ART PETER, AND UPON THIS ROCK I WILL BUILD MY CHURCH; AND THE GATES OF HELL SHALL NOT PREVAIL AGAINST IT" (MATTHEW 16:18)...*

- *HOWEVER, THE BIRTH OF THE "CHURCH AGE" DID NOT HAPPEN UNTIL THE DAY OF PENTECOST (ACTS 2:1).*

- ***THE "CHURCH AGE" IS A MYSTERY, AND IS NOT SEEN IN PROPHECY UNTIL IT IS REVEALED IN THE NEW TESTAMENT (ACTS 2:1, 42; 5:42; 11:26).***

- *THE CROSS AND THE CHURCH DO NOT APPEAR IN "ANCIENT PROPHECY"...THE "CHURCH AGE" IS THAT TIMELESS PERIOD FROM THE PENTACOST TO THE RAPTURE (ACTS 2:1, 1 THESSALONIANS 4:16-17)...HAS BEEN EXTENDED FROM THE FIRST CENTURY TO THE PRESENT.*

- ***HOWEVER IN DUE TIME GOD WILL PERMIT THE POWER TO RETURN TO THE "REVIVED ROMAN EMPIRE" IN A "TEN NATION" KINGDOM FORM (DANIEL 7:7), FOR THE FINAL EVENTS PRECEDING THE SECOND COMING OF CHRIST IN POWER AND GREAT GLORY; TO SET UP HIS EARTHLY KINGDOM (DANIEL 2:44, MATTHEW 24:30, MARK 13:26).***

- *THIS PANORAMA OF PROPHECY IS THE FRAMEWORK INTO WHICH ALL OTHER DETAILED PROPHECIES CAN BE PLACED...**MASTER DANIEL, CHAPTERS TWO AND SEVEN AND YOU WILL HAVE THE BACKBONE OF GOD'S PLAN FOR THE AGES" (GEORGE A. MILES).***

_____

_____

_____

_____

_____

_____

_____

JESUS' OLIVET DISCOURSE
(MATTHEW 24:1-51)

JESUS' OLIVET DISCOURSE WAS HIS LAST MAJOR DISCOURSE, AND HIS MOST PROPHETIC AND APOCALYPTIC MESSAGE REGARDING THE END OF THE WORLD (OR THE AGE).

- *...WHILE THE MESSAGE INCLUDES A PREDICTION OF THE IMMINENT FALL OF JERUSALEM (TITUS, A.D. 70), IT GOES FAR BEYOND THAT; TO POINT US TO THE DISTANT FUTURE, DURING WHICH THE "TIMES OF THE GENTILES" WILL CONTINUE UNTIL THE END OF "THE GREAT TRIBULATION" (DANIEL 7:1-14, MATTHEW 24:29,30).*

THE MOUNT OF OLIVES

- *JESUS LEFT THE CITY OF JERUSALEM AND WENT EAST OF JERUSALEM TO THE "MOUNT OF OLIVES"; FROM WHICH HE COULD LOOK DOWN ON THE TEMPLE COURTYARD...*

THERE HIS DISCIPLES ASKED HIM THREE QUESTIONS:

1. *WHEN SHALL THE DESTRUCTION OF THE TEMPLE BE? (MATTHEW 24:1-2, MARK 13:1-2)...*
2. *AND WHAT SHALL BE THE SIGN OF THY COMING...*
3. *AND OF THE END OF THE AGE? (MATTHEW 24:1-51)*

_____

_____

_____

_____

_____

_____

_____

_____

_____

THESE THREE PROPHETIC QUESTIONS ARE INTERWOVEN; AND SOMETIMES IT IS DIFFICULT TO DETERMINE WHICH EVENT IS BEING DESCRIBED IN JESUS' RESPONSE

- ...THEREFORE, THE ENTIRE OLIVET DISCOURSE MUST BE SEEN AS ANSWERING ALL THREE QUESTIONS.
- MOST PROPHECIES ARE CAPABLE OF BOTH A NEAR AND A REMOTE FULFILLMENT.

THE TEMPLE

1. **SOLOMON'S TEMPLE** (THE ORIGINAL TEMPLE)
   - BUILT 1012 -1005 B.C. (1 KINGS 6:1, 14)...
   - DESTROYED (NEBUCHADNEZZAR) 586 B.C. (2 KINGS 25: 8-9).
2. **ZERUBBABEL'S TEMPLE**
   - RESTORATION OF SOLOMON'S TEMPLE...
   - BUILT BY ZERUBBABEL 520 B.C. (EZRA 3:8; 5:2)
3. **HEROD'S TEMPLE (MATTHEW 24:1-2)**
   - BUILT ABOUT 20-19 B.C., DESTROYED A.D. 70 (TITUS)
   - HAS NOT BEEN RESTORED TO THIS DATE

NOTE!

A MOHAMMAD MOSQUE PRESENTLY RESTS ON THE ORIGINAL TEMPLE SITE.

_____

_____

_____

_____

_____

_____

Jesus' Olivet Discourse
Matthew 24:1-51

Matthew 24:

1. And Jesus went out, and departed from the temple: and his disciples came to him for to shew him the buildings of the temple.

2. And Jesus said unto them, See ye not all these things? verily I say unto you, There shall not be left here one stone upon another, that shall not be thrown down.

3. And as he sat upon the mount of Olives, the disciples came unto him privately, saying, Tell us, when shall these things be? and what shall be the sign of thy coming, and of the end of the world?

4. And Jesus answered and said unto them, Take heed that no man deceive you.

5. For many shall come in my name, saying, I am Christ; and shall deceive many.

6. And ye shall hear of wars and rumours of wars: see that ye be not troubled: for all these things must come to pass, but the end is not yet.

7. For nation shall rise against nation, and kingdom against kingdom: and there shall be famines, and pestilences, and earthquakes, in divers places.

8. All these are the beginning of sorrows.

9. Then shall they deliver you up to be afflicted, and shall kill you: and ye shall be hated of all nations for my name's sake.

10. And then shall many be offended, and shall betray one another, and shall hate one another.

11. And many false prophets shall rise, and shall deceive many.

12. And because iniquity shall abound, the love of many shall wax cold.

13. But he that shall endure unto the end, the same shall be saved.

14. And this gospel of the kingdom shall be preached in all the world for a witness unto all nations; and then shall the end come.

15. When ye therefore shall see the abomination of desolation, spoken of by Daniel the prophet, stand in the holy place, (whoso readeth, let him understand:)

16. Then let them which be in Judaea flee into the mountains:

17. Let him which is on the housetop not come down to take any thing out of his house:

MATTHEW 24:

18.*NEITHER LET HIM WHICH IS IN THE FIELD RETURN BACK TO TAKE HIS CLOTHES.*

19.*AND WOE UNTO THEM THAT ARE WITH CHILD, AND TO THEM THAT GIVE SUCK IN THOSE DAYS!*

20.*BUT PRAY YE THAT YOUR FLIGHT BE NOT IN THE WINTER, NEITHER ON THE SABBATH DAY:*

21.**FOR THEN SHALL BE GREAT TRIBULATION, SUCH AS WAS NOT SINCE THE BEGINNING OF THE WORLD TO THIS TIME, NO, NOR EVER SHALL BE.**

22.**AND EXCEPT THOSE DAYS SHOULD BE SHORTENED, THERE SHOULD NO FLESH BE SAVED: BUT FOR THE ELECT'S SAKE THOSE DAYS SHALL BE SHORTENED.**

23.*THEN IF ANY MAN SHALL SAY UNTO YOU, LO, HERE IS CHRIST, OR THERE; BELIEVE it NOT.*

24.*FOR THERE SHALL ARISE FALSE CHRISTS, AND FALSE PROPHETS, AND SHALL SHEW GREAT SIGNS AND WONDERS; INSOMUCH THAT, IF it were POSSIBLE, THEY SHALL DECEIVE THE VERY ELECT.*

25.*BEHOLD, I HAVE TOLD YOU BEFORE.*

26.*WHEREFORE IF THEY SHALL SAY UNTO YOU, BEHOLD, HE IS IN THE DESERT; GO NOT FORTH: BEHOLD, he is IN THE SECRET CHAMBERS; BELIEVE it NOT.*

27.**FOR AS THE LIGHTNING COMETH OUT OF THE EAST, AND SHINETH EVEN UNTO THE WEST; SO SHALL ALSO THE COMING OF THE SON OF MAN BE.**

28.*FOR WHERESOEVER THE CARCASE IS, THERE WILL THE EAGLES BE GATHERED TOGETHER.*

29.**IMMEDIATELY AFTER THE TRIBULATION OF THOSE DAYS SHALL THE SUN BE DARKENED, AND THE MOON SHALL NOT GIVE HER LIGHT, AND THE STARS SHALL FALL FROM HEAVEN, AND THE POWERS OF THE HEAVENS SHALL BE SHAKEN:**

30.**AND THEN SHALL APPEAR THE SIGN OF THE SON OF MAN IN HEAVEN: AND THEN SHALL ALL THE TRIBES OF THE EARTH MOURN, AND THEY SHALL SEE THE SON OF MAN COMING IN THE CLOUDS OF HEAVEN WITH POWER AND GREAT GLORY.**

31.*AND HE SHALL SEND HIS ANGELS WITH A GREAT SOUND OF A TRUMPET, AND THEY SHALL GATHER TOGETHER HIS ELECT FROM THE FOUR WINDS, FROM ONE END OF HEAVEN TO THE OTHER.*

32.*NOW LEARN A PARABLE OF THE FIG TREE; WHEN HIS BRANCH IS YET TENDER, AND PUTTETH FORTH LEAVES, YE KNOW THAT SUMMER is NIGH:*

33.*SO LIKEWISE YE, WHEN YE SHALL SEE ALL THESE THINGS, KNOW THAT IT IS NEAR, even AT THE DOORS.*

34.*VERILY I SAY UNTO YOU, THIS GENERATION SHALL NOT PASS, TILL ALL THESE THINGS BE FULFILLED.*

35.HEAVEN AND EARTH SHALL PASS AWAY, BUT MY WORDS SHALL NOT PASS AWAY.

36.BUT OF THAT DAY AND HOUR KNOWETH NO man, NO, NOT THE ANGELS OF HEAVEN, BUT MY FATHER ONLY.

37.BUT AS THE DAYS OF NOE were, SO SHALL ALSO THE COMING OF THE SON OF MAN BE.

38.FOR AS IN THE DAYS THAT WERE BEFORE THE FLOOD THEY WERE EATING AND DRINKING, MARRYING AND GIVING IN MARRIAGE, UNTIL THE DAY THAT NOE ENTERED INTO THE ARK,

39.AND KNEW NOT UNTIL THE FLOOD CAME, AND TOOK THEM ALL AWAY; SO SHALL ALSO THE COMING OF THE SON OF MAN BE.

40.THEN SHALL TWO BE IN THE FIELD; THE ONE SHALL BE TAKEN, AND THE OTHER LEFT.

41.Two women shall be GRINDING AT THE MILL; THE ONE SHALL BE TAKEN, AND THE OTHER LEFT.

42.WATCH THEREFORE: FOR YE KNOW NOT WHAT HOUR YOUR LORD DOTH COME.

43.BUT KNOW THIS, THAT IF THE GOODMAN OF THE HOUSE HAD KNOWN IN WHAT WATCH THE THIEF WOULD COME, HE WOULD HAVE WATCHED, AND WOULD NOT HAVE SUFFERED HIS HOUSE TO BE BROKEN UP.

44.THEREFORE BE YE ALSO READY: FOR IN SUCH AN HOUR AS YE THINK NOT THE SON OF MAN COMETH.

45.WHO THEN IS A FAITHFUL AND WISE SERVANT, WHOM HIS LORD HATH MADE RULER OVER HIS HOUSEHOLD, TO GIVE THEM MEAT IN DUE SEASON?

46.BLESSED is THAT SERVANT, WHOM HIS LORD WHEN HE COMETH SHALL FIND SO DOING.

47.VERILY I SAY UNTO YOU, THAT HE SHALL MAKE HIM RULER OVER ALL HIS GOODS.

48.BUT AND IF THAT EVIL SERVANT SHALL SAY IN HIS HEART, MY LORD DELAYETH HIS COMING;

49.AND SHALL BEGIN TO SMITE his FELLOWSERVANTS, AND TO EAT AND DRINK WITH THE DRUNKEN;

50.THE LORD OF THAT SERVANT SHALL COME IN A DAY WHEN HE LOOKETH NOT FOR him, AND IN AN HOUR THAT HE IS NOT AWARE OF,

51.AND SHALL CUT HIM ASUNDER, AND APPOINT him HIS PORTION WITH THE HYPOCRITES: THERE SHALL BE WEEPING AND GNASHING OF TEETH.

PRESENT DAY WORLD DEVELOPMENTS

ISRAEL (JEWS)

1. HOLOCAUST…GERMAN NAZIS' SLAUGHTER OF THE JEWS
2. ESTABLISHMENT OF THE STATE OF "ISRAEL" (1948)
3. TERRITORIAL DISPUTES; OCCUPIED TERRITORY, 1967 WAR, ETC.
4. CURRENT THREATS; RADICAL ISLAMISTS, SURROUNDING NEIGHBORS, TERRORISM

NEW WORLD ORDER

1. GLOBAL ECONOMICS, WORLD MARKETS…
2. THE GROWING INFLUENCE OF THE E.U. (EUROPEAN UNION) IN WORLD AFFAIRS

UNIVERSAL MORAL AND SPIRITUAL DECLINE

1. APOSTASY
2. FALSE DOCTRINE
3. PERSECUTION OF CHRISTIANS
4. RE-DEFINITION OF MARRIAGE AND FAMILY
5. POLITICAL CORRECTNESS
6. INCREASE IN CRIME AND VIOLENCE

NOTE!
AS THE DAYS OF NOAH… (MATTHEW 24:37)

_____

_____

_____

_____

_____

_____

_____

NATURAL DISASTERS

EARTHQUAKES

1. UNITED STATES OF AMERICA
2. JAPAN
3. HAITI
4. THROUGHOUT THE WORLD

FLOODING

1. TORNADOS
2. HURRICANES
3. TSUNAMIS
4. ROARING AND TOSSING OF THE SEAS

SPACE PHENOMENA

1. METEORS
2. METEORITES
3. GLOBAL WARMING...

SUGGESTED READING

1. THE GENTILE INTERLUDE

- ❖ *2 CHRONICLES* _____ *36:5-21*
- ❖ *DANIEL* _____ *2:1-45*
- ❖ *DANIEL* _____ *7:1-14*
- ❖ *REVELATION* _____ *13:1-8*
- ❖ *REVELATION* _____ *19:7-21*
- ❖ *ZECHARIAH* _____ *1:18,19*
- ❖ *LUKE* _____ *21:20-24*
- ❖ *REVELATION* _____ *20:4,7-10*

2. THE CHURCH AGE

- ❖ *MATTHEW* _____ *16:13-18*
- ❖ *ACTS* _____ *2:1,36-42*
- ❖ *ACTS* _____ *5:42*
- ❖ *ACTS* _____ *11:25,26*
- ❖ *I THESSALONIANS* _____ *4:13-17*

3. JESUS' OLIVET DISCOURSE

- ❖ *MATTHEW* _____ *24:1-51*

ABOUT THE AUTHOR

Excerpts from the Author's Autobiography

Reverend S. Elbert Gaffney was born in Gaffney, South Carolina to wonderful Christian parents; the late Warren Gaffney Sr.; and the late Marie Mills Gaffney, who brought him (as well as his eight siblings) up in the nurture and admonition of the Lord.

He accepted Jesus Christ as his personal savior and lord at the age of eleven. Reverend S. Elbert Gaffney's Christian service during the ensuing years include: member: The Gideons International, Deaconship, Pianist/Organist, Sunday School Director, and Minister of the Gospel. Studies/Courses taken to improve his serve include: Biblical Counseling, Experiencing God, Typology, Purpose Driven Life, Death and Dying, Church Growth/Development, Evangelism, Teaching the bible to win the loss and develop the saved.

Professionally, Reverend S. Elbert Gaffney is a Board Certified member of The American Society of Clinical Pathologist. He retired from the Armed Forces Institute of Pathology as a Surgical Pathology Laboratory Supervisor in 1991. He was voted "Technician of the Year" in 1986 by his peers. His scientific publications include: The Gaffney's Giemsa stain (Author), and Laboratory Methods in Histotechnology (Co-Author).

Militarily, Reverend S. Elbert Gaffney served as a Non-Commissioned Officer and squad leader with the U.S Army, Korea, on the DMZ. His decorations include: The Good Conduct Medal, and the Korean Defense Service Medal.

Since retirement from the Armed Forces Institute of Pathology, Reverend S. Elbert Gaffney has devoted his life to full time Christian Service. He currently serves as Associate Minister and Church Organist, at Island Creek Baptist Church, Cowpens South Carolina; under the pastor-ship of Reverend Timothy L. Hunter.

To GOD Be the GLORY!!

MEMBER STATES OF THE EU

(YEAR OF THE ENTRY)

AUSTRIA (1995)
BELGIUM (1952)
BULGARIA (2007)
CROATIA (2013)
CYPRUS (2004)
CZECH REPUBLIC (2004)
DENMARK (1973)
ESTONIA (2004)
FINLAND (1995)
FRANCE (1952)
GERMANY (1952)
GREECE (1981)
HUNGARY (2004)
IRELAND (1973)
ITALY (1952)
LATVIA (2004)
LITHUANIA (2004)
LUXEMBOURG (1952)
MALTA (2004)
NETHERLANDS (1952)
POLAND (2004)
PORTUGAL (1986)
ROMANIA (2007)
SLOVAKIA (2004)
SLOVENIA (2004)
SPAIN (1986)
SWEDEN (1995)
UNITED KINGDOM (1973)

ON THE ROAD TO EU MEMBERSHIP

CANDIDATE COUNTRIES

ICELAND
MONTENEGRO
SERBIA
THE FORMER YUGOSLAV REPUBLIC OF
MACEDONIA
TURKEY

REFERENCES

HOLY BIBLE: KJV, NIV, SCOFIELD, LONG'S CHAIN REFERENCE BIBLE
OTHER REFERENCES
PROPHETIC OUTLINES (GEORGE A. MILES)
SIGNS OF THE TIMES (H.L. WILMINGTON)
INTERNET
GOOGLE IMAGES…
THE EUROPEAN UNION (E.U.)

CPSIA information can be obtained at www.ICGtesting.com
Printed in the USA
LVOW05s1836030115

421379LV00002B/19/P